CHIEF JOSEPH

Leader of Destiny

by Kate Jassem
illustrated by Robert Baxter

Troll Associates

Troll Associates, Mahwah, N.J.

Library of Congress Catalog Card Number: 78-18048
ISBN 0-89375-155-3

CHIEF JOSEPH

Leader of Destiny

CANADA

Bear
Paw Mt.

Colville
Res.

ROCKY

MONTANA

river

WASHINGTON

LOOKOUT PASS

Great Falls

Missouri

M
O
U
N
T
A
I
N
S

Helena

LOLO PASS

Clearwater R.

LAPWAI RES.

WALLA
WALLA

Big Hole R.

Butte

BLUE   WALLOWA   MOUNTAINS

Snake R.

BOZEMAN
PASS

White Bird
Canyon

SALMON

Salmon R.

RIVER

MOUNTAINS

WYO.

OREGON

Snake R.

IDAHO

YELLOWSTONE
NATIONAL
PARK

Joseph awoke with the dawn and shook his little brother, Ollokot.

There was no time to lose. It was the day they had waited for all winter. Today they would ride their spotted ponies to the summer campgrounds.

Quickly, they dressed in their best beaded shirts, leggings, and moccasins. They would ride proudly beside their father, Chief Tu-eka-kas.

Joseph hoped that one day he, too, would be a great Chief.

5

Joseph's father led the smallest but richest band of Nez Percé Indians. His tribe owned great herds of cattle, and raised spotted Appaloosa horses that were the finest and fastest horses anywhere!

All winter they lived snugly in the deep valley between the Blue Mountains and the winding waters of the Snake River.

In springtime, they rode to the plateau, where the hills were bright with wildflowers and sweet berries. They hunted deer, elk, mountain goats, and grizzly bears.

6

Here the river ran silver with salmon. With spears and nets, the Indians fished from dawn to sunset. Many salmon were dried and stored for winter. But the first feast of fresh salmon was always the best!

Joseph and his brother Ollokot were never hungry. Their land of the Wallowa Valley gave them everything they needed.

For as long as Joseph could remember, strangers had been coming to the land of the Nez Percé. It seemed that each summer, more and more wagons rolled across the Oregon prairie.

Chief Tu-eka-kas always had been friendly with the outsiders. Almost fifty years before, Nez Percé Indians had welcomed Lewis and Clark, the explorers who crossed the great Rocky Mountains.

Tu-eka-kas had seen many traders and trappers come and go. He had even given his first son a white man's name, Joseph.

But now many more wagons came, one after another. Soldiers' wagons! Gold miners' wagons! Settlers' wagons!

Some kept going, but many stayed.

In 1855, the soldiers called all the Nez Percé Chiefs to a meeting at Walla Walla. The government wanted to send all the Indians to reservations. Then the land would be used for settlers and farmers.

Joseph saw his father's anger when the Bluecoats offered him blankets and money for his land. His land was not for sale!

When they returned to Wallowa, Tu-eka-kas took Joseph to help him mark their territory with long poles. Now the settlers could make no mistake.

"Inside is the land of our people," he said. "One day you will be Chief, my son. Remember, you must never sell your people's land!"

Joseph did not forget his father's words.

Many years passed in peace. Both Joseph and Ollokot grew tall and strong. The brothers lived in their own tepees now, with wives and children of their own.

On long buffalo hunts to the far plains, they showed courage and skill.

In hunting and sport, the young braves followed Ollokot. But at the council fire, when Joseph spoke, everyone listened. He was not loud and boastful. He was kind but firm. He thought, and then he spoke.

When old Tu-eka-kas died in 1871, his people made Joseph their Chief.

Joseph asked the Great Spirit to let his people live in peace.

10

Each year the settlers moved closer and closer to the Nez Percé homeland. They plowed up new fields. Some stole horses and cattle, and shot any Indian who tried to stop them. With each moon, bad feelings grew between the settlers and Indians.

By then, most of the Nez Percé bands had signed a treaty to leave their land and live on the Lapwai reservation in Idaho. Only Joseph and four other Chiefs stood firm.

Again and again, the Bluecoats' General Howard asked Joseph to move.

In the spring of 1877, Joseph was called to Lapwai. General Howard was no longer asking—he was telling!

He said he would wait thirty days and no more for the Indians to obey. Then, if they did not move peacefully to the reservation, the soldiers would bring them by force.

Chief Joseph had to choose between war and peace.

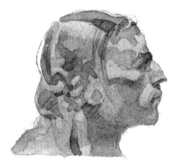

When Joseph returned to Wallowa, he heard the young braves drumming for war.

General Howard had already sent many soldiers. Their guns were ready. Wallowa was surrounded. Joseph knew he had no choice.

At the council fire, Joseph spoke firmly. "We are like deer. They are like the grizzly bear. War will not save our land. We must go to Lapwai."

12

Bravely, the tribe faced the terrible task ahead.

Thousands of their cattle and horses roamed freely. In only thirty days, the Indians had to gather all the herds together. This meant much hard riding over many miles of land.

Their hearts were heavy as they rode their vast homeland for the last time.

The women sadly began to take down their lodges, tying their belongings to travois sleds.

13

Joseph's greatest fear was the river they must cross.

It was spring, and the rushing river churned with melting snow from the mountains. The women and children held fast to the elkskin rafts. Strong warriors on horses guided them to safety.

Not one person was lost to the river!

Next, the horses and cattle were forced to swim.

Horses reared up and ran back to the hills of Wallowa. In the rushing water, many cattle drowned.

Wet and weary, Joseph and his people made camp for the night.

In the morning, Joseph and Ollokot planned to go back across the river, hoping to catch the runaway horses.

While Joseph was gone, most of his people rested for the long journey ahead.

But there were three young braves who could not rest. Leaving their land and horses filled their hearts with anger. One of them had seen his father killed by a settler.

In the stillness of night, they rode away into the darkness.

It was not long before the sky blazed with fire! Guns echoed in the night. By dawn the three young braves had spread terror among the settlers. Eighteen people were dead.

With the sunrise, seventy years of peace between the Nez Percé and the white men had ended.

Now there was no choice. By the time Joseph returned to the camp, his men were dancing and drumming to songs of battle. They knew the Bluecoats would come soon. There would be no talk, only war!

As Chief, he must lead his people.

18

Joseph felt many doubts. He had never before led men into battle. Although he planned for war, he longed for peace.

When the long line of soldiers appeared, Joseph was ready. Half his warriors waited on the slopes of White Bird Canyon.

Joseph gave the signal, and his mounted warriors charged. Their aim was straight. Head-on, they raced toward the Bluecoats!

Quickly, the soldiers turned to retreat. But they did not go far. Ollokot was behind them with his warriors, to finish the fight.

Joseph had won his first battle, but he felt no joy. He knew there was no hope for peace. More Bluecoats would come.

As word of the victory spread, Joseph hurried his people across the Salmon River. He knew the soldiers' wagons would have trouble following them.

Soon, other Nez Percé bands joined Joseph. Together the Chiefs spoke by the council fire. They had little time to lose.

Joseph told them they could stay and fight, but he believed that in the end the Indians would lose. Bluecoats would come in great numbers, like grass in the meadow!

Their only hope was to reach Canada, to the north. It was there that the mighty Sioux Chief, Sitting Bull, had led his people to safety. It was the only way left for the Nez Percé people.

Joseph knew the road would be long and hard. He thought of the dangers of the journey ahead.

He led seven hundred people—but more than half were women, children, and old people. How would they survive the terrible journey through the great mountains and over the wide rivers?

With courage, they climbed the rugged Lolo Pass through the Bitter Root Mountains. It was a rough trail over fallen timber and jagged rocks. There were roaring waterfalls and frightening cliffs that dropped straight down.

Step by step, they made their way through the cold spring rains and chilling winds.

Joseph left a small rear guard behind to watch for the Bluecoats. He knew the soldiers would try to follow.

24

The Indians knew their way through the mountains. They also knew where to find roots and berries for food. Many braves had crossed these wild trails to hunt buffalo.

The soldiers had to carry their food in clumsy wagons. They were cold and hungry. Every day they fell farther and farther behind.

Joseph's men watched, and brought word to their Chief. He knew the first hard leg of their journey was over. Still, many long miles lay ahead.

Joseph's people were tired but happy. They had outrun General Howard, and now they begged Joseph to let them rest in the warm sun of Montana.

There was still a great march ahead, but Joseph was hopeful. He agreed to make camp in the meadow by the Big Hole River. His scouts told him the Bluecoats were many days behind.

But the Bluecoats had more than scouts to carry messages. They could send word on the telegraph wires from one fort to another.

While the Indians rested, General Howard sent a message to Montana. He asked for new troops— men who were rested and fresh.

At dawn, a burst of gunfire and bugles awoke Joseph's camp. Horses charged from every direction.

The Bluecoats had taken the Indians completely by surprise!

In the midst of this sudden, unexpected attack, Joseph took command, shouting orders to his braves.

Quickly, they took up their guns and began to fight. The women and children tried to find cover on the river banks.

Again and again, the soldiers charged. Joseph's warriors aimed straight and true.

At last, the Bluecoats were driven back. The battle was done.

28

Joseph walked sadly among his people. Many loved ones had fallen—his own wife and Ollokot's wife, as well.

With tears of grief, the people of Wallowa again turned toward Canada.

One night, Joseph's scouts brought more bad news. General Howard's men were blocking the way to the north. Something had to be done!

Joseph and Ollokot talked by the campfire. Soon, Ollokot called forty of his best braves together to tell them of a bold plan.

The Indians rode in straight lines past the guards of the Bluecoats' camp. In the darkness, they looked just like soldiers.

In minutes, Ollokot cut the ropes that held the Bluecoats' mules and horses.

A single shot of gunfire rang out.

Shouting and screaming, the warriors started a wild stampede. The plan had worked!

It would take days for the Bluecoats to find their horses. This would give the Indians enough time to get a good head start north.

Joseph led his band through the lands of Yellowstone Park. This was the long way north to Canada, but they hoped it would be safer. Week after week, they pushed on. Their long march became a terrible game of hide and seek.

Once, on the winding trail, they came upon a small party of frightened campers. Joseph would not allow his braves to harm them.

"Our fight is not with these people. We do not kill women and children. We will let them go."

All through the long weeks, Joseph had forbidden his men to harm settlers and their families. They had even traded with some.

In spite of the hardships he had suffered, Joseph had no taste for killing or war. He wished only to lead his people to freedom.

Summer ended early in the north country. The days grew colder, and the nights were bitter.

Ragged and tired, the Indians finally crossed the great Missouri River.

Some felt too tired and sick to go on. Many pleaded for a few days of rest. But Joseph knew they must keep moving.

Far in the distance, he saw the rough peaks of Bear Paw Mountains. From these mountains, they would be just one day's ride to Canada and freedom!

Joseph's hopes soared like an eagle as they reached the dark foothills of the Bear Paw Mountains. One more day—that was all they needed!

Gray storm clouds gathered, and cold October winds whipped through their ragged clothing. The tired travelers pleaded with Joseph to let them rest.

34

Children cried from hunger and cold. Horses were dying.

Now the Indians argued with their leader. Joseph knew they should go on. But there were many who could not make even one more day's ride.

"I would have given my life," Joseph told Ollokot, "rather than to have led this long and terrible march."

Sadly, Joseph agreed to let his people make camp and rest.

Dawn broke with the dreaded sound of gunfire. Suddenly, Bluecoats rushed forward from all sides, shooting wildly at women, children, and warriors.

Joseph shouted commands to his people. They ran to take cover on the hillside.

Again, the Bluecoats had sent messages on the telegraph wires. A new army had come to fight the Nez Percé. The soldiers outnumbered the braves, four to one. Their horses were fresh, and their guns were full.

All day the battle raged. Joseph's men were weary, but still they forced the Bluecoats back, again and again.

Many braves fell that day. Joseph's grief was great when he saw his brother, Ollokot, fall among them.

Now, the cruel cold of night added to their hardships. But Joseph had one last hope. He would not give up.

When it became dark, he sent a small party north, to Canada. His hopes were slim, but maybe, if they hurried, they would reach Chief Sitting Bull of the Sioux. Maybe, he would come back and help Joseph's people.

Again, with the daybreak, the fighting continued. All that day the two sides fought. The cost to the Indians was high. Few braves were left to fight beside him. Joseph knew he could not win. Time was his only hope—time for that small band of riders to reach Sitting Bull!

Joseph knew that if help did not come soon, he would have to surrender.

He waited all night long. No help came.

At sunrise, a white flag was raised in the Indian camp. The guns were silent.

Joseph walked among his people, trying to give them comfort. They had lost many loved ones. They had lost their land. They had come so close to freedom, but now they had lost everything.

At sunset, Joseph rode slowly into the Blue-coats' camp. He rode past a long line of soldiers. His head was bowed as he rode toward the General.

There was silence as he handed his rifle to General Howard.

At last, Joseph raised his face to the sky and spoke. "Hear me, my Chiefs. I am tired. My heart is sick and sad. From where the sun now stands, I will fight no more forever!"

The Indians' long march did not end at Bear Paw. Year after year, they were moved—first to the terrible cold of Dakota, then to the flat, dry heat of Kansas and Oklahoma. Many died on that long trail of tears.

Chief Joseph was a true hero. He had led fewer than three hundred warriors against two thousand soldiers. He had taken his people almost two thousand miles and lost only one battle, thirty miles from freedom.

Joseph kept his word and never fought again. He had been forced into a war he had never wanted. For the rest of his life, he was a great spokesman for his people and for peace among all men.

"I will fight no more forever."